27. Go to the drive-in and watch a really scary movie.

28. Jump up and down on your bed some more.

29. Get down on the floor and lay less than one foot in front of the TV until your eyeballs feel like they are going to bug out.

30. Build a tree house for your kids, big enough for you to fit in.

31. When asking for requests say "please" over and over again until you are out of breath.

32. Attempt to rub your head in a circular motion while patting your stomach.

33. Sing in the shower.

34. Be a little people person; talk to children as much as possible. They are great conversationalists.

35. Go to sleep with a stuffed animal.

36. Make a cake, then sprinkle stuff all over it.

37. Play in the rain.

38. Play in the snow.

39. Fly a kite.

40. Blow bubbles in your milk.

41. Make silly faces in the mirror.

42. Color; buy your own coloring books and crayons. It's easier to stay in the lines now.

43. Play Dress Up.

44. Buy a kiddie meal at a fast food restaurant.

45. Jump on the bed some more.

46. Cut the crust off your sandwich and make a fun shape with your cookie cutter.

47. Write your name on the griddle with pancake batter.

48. Make a face out of your eggs and bacon.

49. Incorporate show and tell into your life.

50. Lay down in your yard on a hot summer's night and look up at the stars.

51. Pitch a tent out in the backyard.

52. Rent whatever your favorite childhood movie was and watch it in the dark, less than one foot away from the TV.

53. Ask the question, "Why?" a lot.

54. Keep jumping on
the bed.

55. Splash in the bathtub.

56. Skip from the kitchen to the living room, be careful doing this one in public.

57. Listen to the same song over and over again.

58. Sing out loud to your favorite song in the car. Who cares what your fellow drivers think, you're having fun.

34

59. Tell spooky stories on a stormy night by candlelight.

60. Think about what you want to be when you grow up.

61. Jump up and down for no reason.

62. Lay down in the grass on a sunny day until you start to itch.

63. Walk around barefoot as often as you can.

64. Turn off the TV and go outside and play.

65. Wrap up presents over and over again into one giant present.

66. Watch your favorite Christmas movies in the middle of the summer.

67. Bring home a giant cardboard box and perform a puppet show for your kids.

68. On the way home from work, stop and buy everyone a surprise.

69. Spend an afternoon looking for a four leaf clover.

70. Climb a tree.

71. Sit in the front row at the movie theater.

72. Smile a lot.

73. Listen to what children have to say.

74. Put your hands on your hips and act like a superhero.

75. Upon answering the phone say, "Hello..Hello?" until the person on the other line is screaming.

76. Play hooky from work and go to the park.

77. Run with arms extended as if you are an airplane.

78. Eat chocolates.

79. Have a
secret handshake.

80. Climb in at the foot of the bed under the sheets.

81. Dress up as the Easter Bunny, Santa, etc.

82. Act like you're really afraid when a child tries to scare you.

83. Save up your change in a piggy bank. Then sit on the floor and count it.

84. Take a field trip.

85. Read comic books.

86. Sit on the floor as much as possible.

87. Daydream in the middle of the day for at least thirty minutes.

88. When riding a bike, pop a "wheelie", even if it's just a little one.

89. Jump on the bed some more.

90. Turn up the stereo really loud and play the air guitar. Sing and dance until someone walks in on you and looks at you like you're nuts.

91. Use the comics to wrap up presents.

92. Have your birthday at a kiddie theme restaurant.

93. Play putt-putt golf at least twice a year.

94. Continue to ask "Why?" a lot.

95. Send yourself flowers. When asked who sent them, reply "Someone who loves me."

96. Have your mom and dad tell you stories about when you were little.

97. Make up wonderful make-believe stories to tell your children every night.

98. Take your children to nursing homes. Those who are truly young at heart will be easily met.

99. Stick your head out of the car window like a dog.

100. Write your name in the sand.

101. Seize every minute of every day. Play till you drop.

102. Buy walkie-talkies even if you don't have children.

103. Wake up on Saturdays like it was Christmas.

104. Learn how to juggle.

105. Blow bubbles with your gum.

106. Play in the mud.

58

107. Stand out in the rain and catch raindrops with your tongue.

108. Pick up things with your toes.

109. Stop jumping on the bed by flinging yourself down with a big sigh.

110. Write a letter to Santa Claus with your children's help and mail it.

111. Buy whatever it was that you wanted as a child that you did not have.

112. Scream at the top of your lungs for no apparent reason. Be careful doing this one in public.

113. Learn to play whatever instrument you always dreamed of knowing how to play.

114. Act like pirate and say "Arrrrrrrrrrrrrr," until you annoy friends and family.

115. Buy little red and gold stars and stick them on work well done.

116. When in the supermarket step on only the black or white squares.

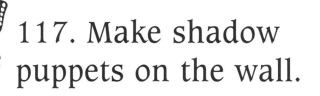

117. Make shadow puppets on the wall.

118. Stand to the right of the doorway and amaze your friends and family by leaning your upper body forward with your arms stretched out like you're flying.

119. Tell jokes as often as possible, but not at another's expense.

120. Build or buy a playhouse for the backyard.

121. Speak in pig Latin.

122. Watch the Three Stooges.

123. Give yourself an allowance and spend it only on yourself.

124. Take off from work on your birthday.

125. Celebrate your birthday the entire week.

126. Start jumping on the bed again.

127. Let your heart be the first thing you listen to.

128. Pick a dandelion; make a wish and blow off all the fuzzy stuff.

129. Play beauty shop on a Saturday night.

130. Go to restaurants that offer crayons and paper tablecloths, as a masterpiece is waiting to happen.

131. Try to roll your tongue and flip your eyelids up.

132. Make strange sounds when your hand is strategically placed in your armpit.

133. Perform magic tricks.

134. While traveling repeatedly ask, "Are we there yet?"

135. When standing next to someone for a photograph, give them rabbit ears with your fingers.

136. Go roller skating.

74

137. Be a big brother or sister to a child.

138. Talk on the phone to a friend till your ear feels like it might fall off.

139. Make arrangements to have a neighborhood carnival or block party.

140. Decorate like a maniac on all major holidays.

141. Go for a nature walk.

142. Go through all your school work and report cards, if you're fortunate enough to still have them.

143. Keep jumping on the bed.

144. Eat candy that turns your tongue strange colors.

145. Arm wrestle.

146. Play childhood games with your children.

147. Tell children about the day they were born as often as they want to hear it.

148. Make your own greeting cards; a gift made by your own hands is still a treasured gift.

149. Buy the new and improved oozie water guns. They're tons better than when we were young.

150. Make an effort to keep up with what slang is popular with children now. Then try to incorporate it into your vocabulary.

151. When asked a difficult question, play Scarlett and think about it tomorrow.

152. Learn how to do impressions of people.

153. When opening a present, rip through it and don't try to save the wrapping paper.

154. Have a pillow fight.

155. Always plan out a great April Fool's and get as many people as you can.

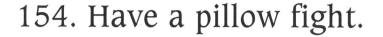

156. Play Santa Claus to a family who is down on their luck every year.

157. Have an open heart and mind.

158. Continue jumping on the bed.

159. Trace your hand on a piece of paper, then turn it into a turkey.

160. Play "paper, rock, scissors" and "one potato, two potato" to settle a dispute.

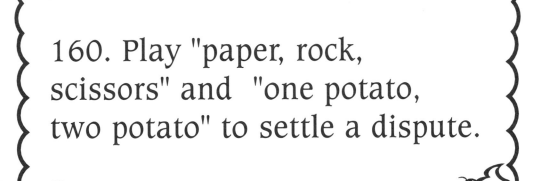

161. Send yourself a singing telegram and act like you don't know who sent it.

162. Contact your very best friend and plan a special reunion.

163. Help children learn
to avoid the same mistakes
that you made.

164. Wear a little
party hat on your
birthday and
look ridiculous.

89

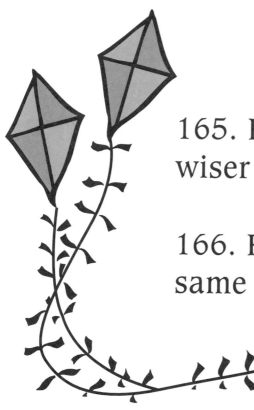

165. Play dolls as older, wiser women.

166. Play army the same way.

167. Buy a little license plate with your name on it for your bike.

168. Talk in really silly voices.

169. Try to figure out what something really strange is on the sidewalk.

170. Ask for twenty dollars worth of quarters.

171. Wear a snorkel and mask in the swimming pool until it is permanently suctioned to your face.

172. Stay in the bath tub until you get prune-y.

173. Sprawl out on the living room floor with your favorite blanket less than one foot away from the TV.

174. Repeat jumping on the bed.

175. Stick your tongue out and place your thumbs in your ears while wiggling your fingers.

176. To an unreasonable demand say, "Uh!" and stomp out of the room mumbling under your breath.

177. Dance in your home or in public, even if you can't dance.

178. Wear clothes that you really want to wear.

179. Use your own generation's slang while discussing current events.

180. Buy school supplies at the end of the summer.

181. Watch wrestling on TV.

182. Have a rubber ducky in the bathroom at all times.

183. Invite friends and family members to jump on the bed.

184. Tell everyone you know and those you don't, that your birthday is tomorrow.

185. Continue trying to figure out what the strange stuff is on the sidewalk.

186. Pick up bugs.

187. Ride down a water slide at least twice a year.

188. Dance around while doing mundane chores.

189. Have a gleam in your eye and a pirate's smile.

190. Draw pictures or doodles
     then proudly put them
     on the refrigerator door.

191. Write your name or someone's name that you love over and over again.

192. Pretend.

193. Buy a bunch of balloons and let them go.

194. Catch lightening bugs in a glass container. Take them into a room with no light and be amazed.

195. Ask for ketchup with everything you eat.

196. When alone in an elevator, tap dance.

197. Swim immediately after eating.

198. Have a picnic on the living room floor, less than one foot away from the TV.

199. Upon seeing a penny on the ground always pick it up.

200. When someone says, "No way," reply, "Yes way."

201. At the sight of seeing something really disgusting, reply, "Oouuuuuuuu."

202. Shove as many french fries as you can get into your mouth.

203. Eat food with your fingers, then wipe them off on your pants.

204. Do a cannon ball into the swimming pool. Repeat until a wave effect begins.

205. When in freezing cold water, act like it's not cold at all.

112

206. Do a forward roll in the front yard.

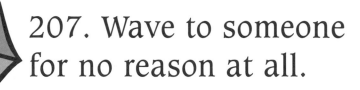

207. Wave to someone for no reason at all.

208. Tell a stranger it is great to see them. They will try to remember who you are for a week.

209. When asked what you might like for dinner, always reply, "Pizza."

210. Never be too tired or too busy when asked to do something fun.

211. Make an angel in the snow.

212. Wink at people.

213. Make homemade
ice cream.

214. When speaking to small children and animals, sound ridiculous.

215. Say, "Shazam!" in an authoritative tone.

216. Smush your face against the car window.

217. Very rarely be still.

218. Upon going to bed, act silly for no apparent reason.

219. Ride the double Ferris wheel at the carnival.

220. Jump in rain puddles.

221. Throw as much change as you have into a fountain and make a wish.

222. Make new best friends.

223. Eat a banana and peanut butter sandwich.

224. Visit your grade school teachers and let them see how their efforts turned out.

225. Run around in circles; roll your eyeballs upwards and place your tongue in the corner of your mouth while making strange sounds.

226. Go skinny dipping.

124

227. Laugh a lot.

228. Jump off the curb with two feet. Upon landing, act as if you jumped from a two story building.

229. Wear your hair in pigtails.

230. Walk around on your knees to see what the view is like.

231. Use exclamation points a lot!!!

232. If someone denies a request, drive them crazy until they say, "yes."

233. Trade something you love for something your best friend loves.

234. When riding a bus, run to get to the very back seat first.

130

235. Race anyone who will race you.

236. When asked how old you are, tell them proudly. Then say you feel twenty.

237. Write love letters.

238. Recite poems that rhyme.

239. Play chopsticks on the piano.

240. Place pennies on your elbow, then try to catch them in the palm of your hand.

241. When telling a story, demand that everyone be quiet and listen to you.

242. Make up nicknames for your friends.

135

243. Refer to cows as "moo-cows": and horses as "horsies."

244. Don't take life, friends, or family for granted.

245. Laugh at yourself and with yourself.

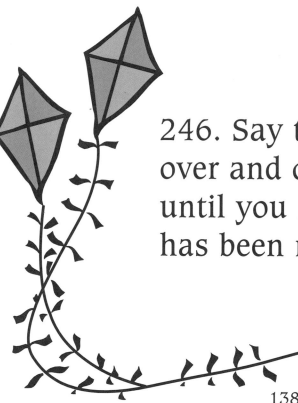

246. Say the same thing over and over again until you feel your point has been made.

247. Take the person you love out in a limo and pretend it's prom night.

248. Jump on a trampoline.

249. Have somebody you love make it all better.

250. Buy gum out of red candy machines.

251. Lay a race or train track down the length of your living room.

252. Shove cotton candy into your mouth.

142

253. Blow spitballs across the table.

254. Decrust white bread, sculpt into a strange shape, then pop it into your mouth.

255. Sing along to commercials, especially the really bad ones.

256. Make smiley faces when you sign your name.

257. Glue macaroni to a paper plate, paint, then proudly display on the refrigerator.

258. Stretch gum out of your mouth, wrapping it around your finger, then chew gum again for more enjoyment.

259. Ask for lollipops at the drive–through teller.

260. Give someone "cooties" then give them a "cootie shot."

261. Make-believe.

262. Triple dog dare someone.

263. Volunteer at your local children's hospital.

264. Spill something, then begin to cry.

265. Cry for no reason at all, then suddenly stop.

148

266. Keep your money wadded up in your front pocket.

267. Wear cowboy boots and hat with shorts. Beg your spouse to let you wear them to the grocery store.

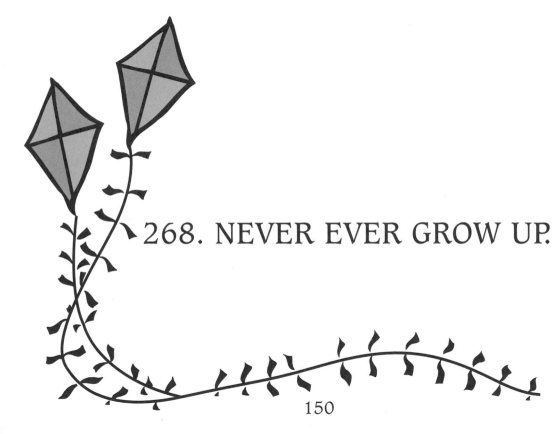

268. NEVER EVER GROW UP.

269. Part your hair to the side on Sundays.

270. Wake up at 5:00 a.m. on Christmas morning.

271. Consider gifts as cashing in on the loot.

272. Remember what your mother told you.

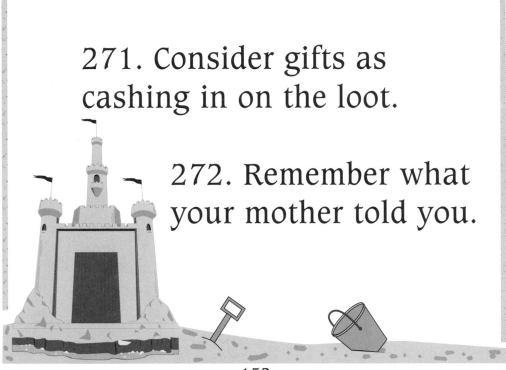

273. Wear something that completely does not match.

274. Tuck your napkin into your collar.

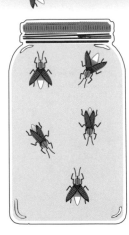

275. Be aware of how beautiful and precious babies are.

276. Attempt to balance things on your nose.

154

277. When placing things into the trash, act like a pro basketball player.

278. Drink an entire soda, then burp really loud.

279. In the company of someone who is really mean make strange faces behind their back. Do not attempt this on your boss.

280. Fall into large piles of leaves until you itch.

281. Play with your dog until you itch.

282. Mow someone's yard for money.

283. Mow your parents' yard for no charge at the beginning and end of each season.

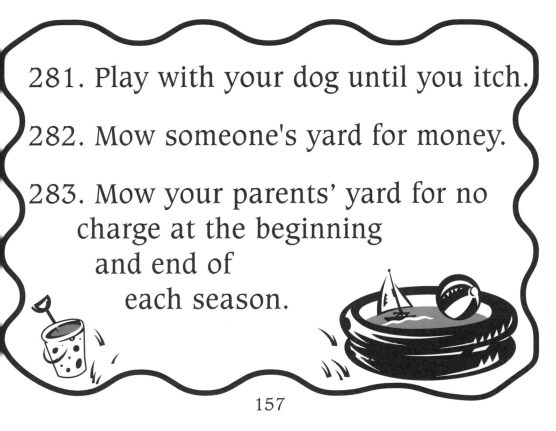

284. Go to a laser light show at your local planetarium.

285. Have grown-up toys.

286. Tell the people you love that you love them.

287. Write a play for your friends and family to perform on Thanksgiving.

288. Have a tea party.

289. Paint a face on
     your stomach.

290. Take a nap.

291. Get an old pot and make a magic potion out of things you find in the back yard.

292. Take a time out when you are upset.

293. Have a blankie. Refrain from going to sleep without it.

294. Learn new things.

295. Believe that
anything is possible.

296. Collect money for a worthy cause.

297. Put straws up your nose.

298. Get incredibly excited when you see people you love.

299. Play "grown-up."

300. Have candles on your cake for every year of your life.

301. Make a wish on the first star you see tonight.

Other Titles By Great Quotations

301 Ways to Stay Young At Heart
African-American Wisdom
A Lifetime of Love
A Light Heart Lives Long
A Servant's Heart
A Teacher Is Better Than Two books
A Touch of Friendship
Angle-grams
As A Cat Thinketh
Astrology for Cats
Astrology for Dogs
Can We Talk
Celebrating Women
Chicken Soup
Chocoholic Reasonettes
Daddy & Me
Erasing My Sanity
Fantastic Father, Dependable Dad
Golden Years, Golden Words
Graduation Is Just The Beginning
Grandma, I Love You
Happiness Is Found Along The Way
High Anxieties
Hooked on Golf

I Didn't Do it
Ignorance Is Bliss
I'm Not Over the Hill
Inspirations
Interior Design for Idiots
Let's Talk Decorating
Life's Lessons
Life's Simple Pleasures
Looking for Mr. Right
Midwest Wisdom
Mother, I Love You
Motivating Quotes,
    for Motivated People
Mommy & Me
Mrs. Murphy's Laws
Mrs. Webster's Dictionary
My Daughter,
    My Special Friend
Only A Sister
Parenting 101
Pink Power
Reflections
Romantic Rhapsody
Social Disgraces

Someone Pleeease pull
    The Fire Alarm!
Stress or Sanity
TeenAge of Insanity
Thanks From The Heart
The ABC's of Parenting
The Be-Attitudes
The Cornerstone of Success
The Lemonade Handbook
The Mother Load
The Other Species
The Rose Mystique
The Secrets in Your face
The Secrets in Your Name
The Secret Language of men
The Secret Language of
    Women
The Sports Page
Things You'll Learn...
Wedding Wonders
Word From The Coach
Working Woman's World

Great Quotations, Inc.

8102 Lemont Road,
#300, Woodridge, IL 60517
Phone: 630-985-2628   Fax: 630-985-2610